ON WINGS OF SILVER DREAMS

SRI CHINMOY

ISBN 0-88497-4991-1

Printed and Published by
AUM PUBLICATIONS
86-24 Parsons Blvd.
Jamaica, N.Y. 11432

Introduction

Inherently fascinating, often inspiring, yet intangible and illusory are our dreams. With their prophetic messages, dreams have the capacity to offer us deep inner wisdom and vision. They may foretell the future, warn us of disastrous events, reveal the solution to a problem or bless us with a spiritual experience. Our hearts are healed by dreaming of a beloved friend or family member. We long to live constantly in the dream worlds of peace and joy.

But there is the darker side of dreams. Frightening nightmares destroy our sleep and even disturb our waking hours. demons pursue us; we find ourselves caught in menacing worlds, unable to move, unable to see, unable to cry out for help. We awaken in terror and wonder what we could have done, either consciously or unconsciously to have brought such dreams into our sleep. For weeks we may feel the effects of these bad dreams.

How can our dream-world-friend be so unpredictable? One moment we are given uplifting visions that raise us to the higher worlds, and the next moment dreadful spectres from lower realms attack us. How can we decipher the fragmented dreams that come to us—and more importantly, is deciphering dreams even a worthwhile pursuit?

This collection of Sri Chinmoy's answers guides us through the confusing labyrinth, teaching us how to understand the significance of some common dreams and also how gain some control over the kinds of dreams we have. With the knowledge obtained from reading this book, we can better assimilate the blessing-gifts of inspiration and aspiration from our visionary dreams, and with our purity and inner strength we can laugh at the goblins-of-the-dark that try to capture us in our nightmares.

At last we can all sleep in peace.

Anupadi

On my silver dream's wings
Every night I fly.

What is a dream?

Today's dream is tomorrow's reality. Why? Because a dream comes from a world which is living and palpable. With our limited consciousness we may not know this, but when we meditate we consciously enter into many higher worlds. The reality of these worlds enters into us in our dreams.

What we call a dream here on earth, in some other world is a reality. It is a reality in its own right, but when it comes to us, we are a stranger to it and it is a stranger to us. When we have a dream it is like two strangers meeting for the first time. Since they do not know each other, they may be very puzzled or astonished by each other. But once they start living together, they do not remain strangers anymore. In the beginning, when the reality first comes and touches the earth plane where we live, we feel that it is a dream. But if we go to its source, we will see that it is already a reality there. And when the dream stays with us for some time, then it becomes a reality here as well.

An ordinary person sees a dream as something totally separate from the rest of his life. He feels that he is living in the reality, whereas the dream has nothing to do with reality. It is something sweet, something precious, something encouraging, something inspiring and so forth, but he does not feel that it is more than that. But when a spiritual person has a dream, he can immediately feel that his dream is the precursor of reality. He feels that each dream is a stepping-stone toward his divine Goal.

Where do dreams come from?

There are many worlds which are not visible to our human eyes, and dreams come from those worlds. Some dreams take place in the vital plane. These dreams are very often confusing, because there is not much light in the vital, which is the world of enjoyment. In dreams from the vital world there are many sensations and great excitement. Dreams that come from the higher worlds are luminous, but they have no sensations in them. When we get a dream from the vital plane, we will see constant movement. It will be like a battlefield where everything is being broken and smashed, and people are being killed. When we have dreams coming from the lower worlds, the subconscious, or you can say inconscient worlds, we have to feel that these dreams have no value. They cannot change our nature. They cannot inspire us. They cannot give us any hope for our future fulfilment. The best thing we can do is forget them.

If a dream comes from the mental plane, there will be some poise—not full poise, but a little poise, a little calm and quiet. If it comes from the psychic plane, we will feel affection, sweetness, compassion and concern for the things or persons we are seeing. And if it comes from the soul's plane, it will be all light, delight and peace.

When we have a dream from the lower worlds, we may not want to identify ourselves with it, for we may be badly frightened by it. The dream comes to us as a threat. But a dream that comes from the higher worlds comes as an invitation. These dreams are harbingers of reality. We get inner joy and inner satisfaction and immediately feel our identity there. Then we have to enter into that reality and grow into it.

If we meditate, we can consciously enter into the dream worlds. Right now, to us the dream worlds are something vague, uncertain and to some extent obscure. But if we study them, we can know many things about them.

Can we learn from our dreams?

We can learn much from our dreams, but we have to know from which plane of consciousness a dream is coming. If it comes from the lower vital plane, then we have to discard it. If we have a dream that somebody is killing us or that we are killing someone, it is absurd to pay attention to it. Dreams from the lower vital plane are unimportant and useless. There is nothing to be learned from them.

But if the dream comes from the intuitive plane, from the psychic plane, from the higher mind, from the overmind, from the illumined mind, then we have to give it importance. If we see that we have the capacity or the need to help someone in his meditation or elevate his consciousness, then to that kind of dream we have to pay proper attention.

The dreams that come to us from a higher plane, good dreams, divine dreams, we have to treasure. When we have this kind of dream, we can try to expedite their transformation into reality. As spiritual persons, as seekers, we want to create peace. That should be our highest dream. We will invoke peace from above and then offer peace to mankind. So our higher dreams, divine dreams, are most welcome, but destructive dreams, lower vital dreams, have to be discarded.

What determines what we dream?

Your inner beings, your aspiration and the entire universe inside your spiritual heart determine what you dream. But if your aspiring heart is not big enough for you to identify with the Universal Consciousness, then you will feel that things are coming from the outside. Your aspiring heart can be made bigger only through increased aspiration. There comes a time when the aspiring heart becomes one with the Universal Heart, which is flooded with light and delight. It is this Heart that determines all encouraging dreams from the most significant to the most insignificant.

When I am asleep, who is it that sees my dreams?

There is no hard and fast rule that one particular inner reality observes the sleep state or the dreams that you are having. When you are asleep, one of your inner beings can see your dreams, or the aspiration accumulated in your inner life can watch your sleep and observe your dreams, or the divine Grace and Compassion which wants to manifest itself in and through you can do it.

*Does our highest consciousness continue to oper-
ate while we sleep?*

When we sleep, sometimes our highest con-
sciousness continues to operate and sometimes it
does not. It depends on whether God wants the
highest consciousness to operate or whether God
wants the highest consciousness to sleep while the
physical is taking rest. It entirely depends on
God's Will.

There are many seekers who meditate sincerely
every day. Just because they have meditated dur-
ing the day, God is pleased with them and God
says to them, "My children, you have worked
very hard. During the day, you have prayed and
meditated. Now I have other instruments that
can most powerfully help you. Now there are
other forces that can work on your behalf."

At that time, He asks the higher self or the
higher beings to operate and help the seekers who
prayed and meditated during the day. But if we
don't pray and meditate during the day, God will
never ask the higher forces to work for us. Only
when the Inner Pilot is pleased with the seeker
will He ask the higher forces to help when the
person is asleep.

If you awaken with a feeling of elation and joy, does this mean you had a spiritual experience during a dream although your physical mind may not remember it?

It is quite possible. You may not remember it because your physical consciousness may not have a free access to the particular plane of consciousness where you have had the experience. After you have an experience, you have to come down through various descending rungs of consciousness before entering into your ordinary waking consciousness. If you are only a beginner in the spiritual life, there may be no link between the first rung and the rung where you had the experience. If you remain in the physical consciousness during the day, then the experience that you have had in the inner world cannot function properly. The physical consciousness must be surcharged with the divine light; then only will it be able to have a free access to all the planes of consciousness.

When you sleep, the soul moves freely from this plane to that plane like a bird. If the physical wants to observe what the soul is doing, then the physical has to be moulded and guided by the soul's light. Often you cannot bring these experiences into your conscious memory because you are not aware of all the stages that exist between the higher plane and the physical plane. The best way to become more conscious and open is to spend more time in meditation. If you now meditate for one hour a day, then try to spend two hours a day. God has given you twenty-four hours. Out of this time you can spend more time in meditation. In silence you can speak to God more, in silence He can act more powerfully in and through you.

Could you speak a little more about how the soul flies to different planes during sleep?

There are three states of consciousness. *Susupti*, which you can call the dreamless state, is the purest, deepest, highest sleep. Then there is *swapan*, the dream state, and finally *jagriti*, wakefulness. In deep sleep the soul gets the opportunity to fly from one plane of consciousness to another. We have many layers of consciousness inside our being, but when we are working, talking and mixing with others in the hustle and bustle of the world, the inner being is crushed and the soul does not get the opportunity to fly. When we are in the outer world and all kinds of things come into our outer mind, it is all restlessness. But in deep sleep, the entire being is silenced and the soul can fly like a bird from one plane of consciousness to another. When the soul makes this flight without any obstruction, all the doors and windows in our inner being are automatically opened. When the inner doors are all open and the soul is flying, at that time the outer being becomes one with the Divine and experiences the consciousness of delight.

When we dream, do our souls visit many different planes of consciousness, or do they usually visit the same planes?

When we dream, our souls visit many different planes of consciousness. Our soul is like a bird. Now it sits on one branch, later it can sit on another branch and the next moment it can sit on a third branch. Every time we have a dream, there is the possibility for our soul to enter into different planes of consciousness. If the soul wants to, it can enter one particular plane many times. But, like us, the soul enjoys variety. It likes to visit different states of consciousness. Novelty gives us joy; so also in the case of the soul. By visiting new planes of consciousness it acquires more light and, at the same time, offers its own light. There is mutual giving and taking.

How do dreams materialise? Can they be prevented from doing so?

There is no hard and fast rule. You have to know what kinds of dreams they are. Sometimes they are all imaginary dreams which come from the subconscient plane. Let us say that you want to eat chicken, but you don't get any. At night that desire may be transmitted into a dream and in the dream you will be eating chicken. That kind of dream is not a real dream. It is only an unfulfilled desire which comes from the subconscient plane.

When a dream takes place in the mental world, the dream has to come to the vital world for manifestation before it comes to the physical world. The physical world is the last world in which we see it.

But it often happens that an incident may take place in the mental world which never takes place in the physical world. If the vital world resents it, it can prevent this incident from taking place. The vital is like a guard or soldier. If the vital allows it, then that particular incident eventually takes place in the physical world also. But many times dreams are destroyed in the vital world before they reach the physical plane.

Dreams need an opening to enter into the vital, and from there, if they get another opening, they enter into the physical. When the vital opens its door, the incident in the dream comes to the physical and materialises. It is the same with a disease. First it takes place in the deeper or higher regions, and then, when the vital allows it, it takes place in the gross physical. If a disease enters into the mind, it can be prevented from entering into the physical.

Dreams from the vital world very often quickly take form in the physical world because the vital world is closest to the physical world. When we have dreams in the higher regions, in the soul's world, they usually take a long time to manifest in the physical.

A dream that comes from the subconscious world, where we are quarrelling and fighting and doing many undivine things, will not necessarily materialise. But a dream that comes from the higher worlds is like a seed which is bound to germinate in the course of time.

Dreams which we get in the small hours of the morning, between 3:00 and 4:00, at the *Brahma Muhurta* or Hour of God, are likely to materialise, but these dreams have to be properly guarded against impure thoughts. Also, if you have dreams during a lunar eclipse or a solar eclipse, these dreams are usually fulfilled.

Very often we have dreams which we do not recollect in the morning, but the incident that took place is most authentic and it will eventually materialise. Again, there are many things which do not actually first take shape or form in the mental or psychic world. Many incidents can come into being directly from the Universal Consciousness. When the physical can expand its consciousness, like the wings of a bird, many things happen. It can draw experiences directly from the Universal Consciousness, without passing through the mind or the vital. Also, if you want to negate anything in the mental world, you have to be able to enter into the Universal Consciousness and draw energy from there. Once you have free access to the Universal Consciousness, you can go and fight on the mental plane and be successful there.

Does the soul have anything to do with the manifestation of our dreams?

If they are dreams from the lower worlds, the soul will either try to illumine and elevate them or try to destroy them. Unillumined dreams may create tremendous problems for us. If they are undivine dreams, the soul's light fights with them and does not want them to manifest.

If they are elevating dreams, dreams from the higher worlds, then the soul's light expedites their earthward journey. When the realities of the higher worlds want to come down, the soul's light helps them. As a matter of fact, it pulls them like a magnet and tries to manifest them. If they are not manifested, it means that the time has not yet come, or perhaps the Divine within us feels it is necessary for them to be manifested, or the Divine within us may change the game and decide that they should not be manifested.

Do dreams have anything to do with ambition?

Dreams can easily have much to do with ambition. There are two types of ambition. One is the ambition of world-conquerors like Napoleon, Caesar and Alexander the Great. When Caesar said, "I came, I saw, I conquered," that was vital ambition. But spiritual ambition will say, "I saw, I loved, I became." With vital ambition we try to trample others and dominate others, but with spiritual ambition we try to become inseparably and universally one with others.

In the outer world, let us say you are a pilot. When you fly, at that time if you feel that your consciousness is flying in the sky of Infinity and Eternity, then you are bringing to the fore something infinite. But if your ambition is only to go from one place on earth to another, then your goal is limited. It is not an ever-transcending Goal. So if you dream of doing something expanding, something transcending, that kind of dream embodies spiritual ambition. But if the dream has its start and conclusion, if you know your final destination, then that dream cannot take you very far. The ambition that binds you and the ambition that frees you, liberates you, or gives you a sense of Infinity are two different ambitions. When you have a dream, try to feel whether you are entering into the worlds of beauty, peace, light and bliss where everything is constantly growing in infinite measure and where everything is transcending its own reality. If you have that kind of dream, if you have that kind of ambition, then your earth-life can be meaningful and fruitful, and you will become a chosen instrument of the Supreme, for the Supreme.

How important are dreams?

It entirely depends on our necessity. If we need a dream in order to inspire us to go deep within or to go far beyond the mind, then dreams are of paramount importance. Divine dreams, spiritual dreams, can play a considerable role in our spiritual life. Also, we have to know that everything is a dream before it is manifested in the world of reality. If we value the reality, then we have to value the dream as well. But this does not mean that we have to have millions of dreams in order to have God-realisation. No! If we have only a few significant dreams or even if we do not have any dreams, this will not stand in the way of our spiritual progress.

Does knowledge of our dreams help us know God?

Yes, if they are good dreams, if they are inspiring dreams, certainly it helps. But if they are undivine dreams, it will not help. If somebody is stabbing you, if you are in the battlefield or if some catastrophe is taking place, you have to know that these kinds of dreams come from the vital world and they will not help you at all. But if you have a dream in which an angel appears before you, or if your spiritual Master is blessing you in a dream, or if you see a sea of peace right in front of you, then remembering this kind of dream will naturally expedite your spiritual progress. So it depends on what kind of dream you have. Dreams that come from the destructive vital world, cannot help you make any progress. But you can definitely make progress when you see divine things or feel in the dream itself peace, light and bliss in boundless measure.

Should we try to bring our dreams into our meditation?

If you have very happy and delightful dreams, then they may encourage you and inspire you to meditate. Again, it may happen that after you have a dream you will go on imagining all that happened in your dream, even during your meditation. You may say to yourself, "I saw a beautiful Golden Shore." Then you will just remain in the world of your mental recollection and your inner cry will not come to the fore. If you have a very high dream and try to remain there, the intensity of your meditation may go away. Instead, when you have an inspiring dream, remind yourself that the Golden Shore is not a mere dream but a reality and say, "Let me work very hard. Let me meditate most sincrely so that I can go high, higher, highest in reality and not only in the dream-world."

Are there any people who do not have dreams?

There is not a single human being on earth who has not had any dreams. There are some people who say they do not have any dreams at all, but they are mistaken. They do dream, but when they wake up they totally forget them. Other people have the capacity to retain the memory of their dreams while they are fully awake.

Why can't I remember my dreams for more than a split second after waking, even if I try?

There are two main reasons why you do not remember your dreams. One is that you may not give adequate importance to them. You have lost something and you want to get it back, but you are not trying your best. You are not offering your utmost sincere effort to find the thing that you have lost. There is no intensity in your search.

When you have a dream, you may feel that it is only your mental hallucination and nothing else. Also, you may feel that these experiences are nothing unusual, that others also get them. Whether others have dreams or not is not your business. Your business is only to have dreams and, with the help of these dreams, to get a new life and run toward your destined Goal.

If you do not give due value to your dreams, the dreams find that they are not needed, so they do not come and knock at your door. When we give proper value to someone or something, that person or thing remains with us, in us and for us. You will remember your dreams only if you feel that these dreams are of tremendous value. If you have that kind of feeling, then when you forget your dreams, you will feel a sense of tremendous loss, irreparable loss. Then the next time you dream, you will not forget your experiences.

The other reason is that it may not be the Will of God that you remember your dreams. Perhaps you had a bad dream, an unaspiring dream, a frightening dream. The Supreme feels that by remembering this undivine, frightening dream you will gain nothing, absolutely nothing. On the contrary, if you remember that bad dream and think of it for a few hours, it will create fear in you and will ruin your inner aspiration.

Again, if you get a very high, lofty dream and if the Supreme sees that you are unable to assimilate it, He will not allow you to remember it. If He sees that you will become bloated with conscious or unconscious pride and say, "Oh, I had such a lofty dream, I am so great!" then He just takes it away from your conscious mind. He wants you to keep it inside the very depth of your heart, and gradually, gradually He allows the seed to grow inside you. In the course of time it will germinate and grow into a huge tree. When it is a tiny plant, there is a great risk that it may be destroyed by you or by others. But when it become a full-grown tree, it cannot be destroyed. At that time there will not be any pride in you. When you become a mature tree full of delicious fruits, you will humbly bend down and offer these fruits to others.

I very rarely have dreams. If this means I am not remembering them, should I try to remember?

If you don't have dreams often, that means you don't need them. But if you have dreams which you forget when you wake up, then you can try to gain them back. In order to do that, you have to feel that your life is not a reality devoid of dreams. Also you have to know that each divine dream is the clear indication of an imminent reality. If you value the dream as you would value the reality, then an inner being of yours will help you remember your dreams.

How can we remember our dreams when we awaken?

If you feel that you have had a dream but you cannot remember it, then try to concentrate on the back of your head, just at the top of the neck. When you have dreams, either they will manifest through your physical mind, or for some time, for a few hours or even for a day or two, they will be registered at that spot on the back of your head. So if you want to recollect any dream, try to concentrate there and feel that you are knocking at a door. When that door opens, you will be able to remember your dreams completely.

How important is it for us to remember our dreams?

If you have bad dreams, do not try to remember them at all. On the contrary, forget about them immediately! The sooner you forget, the better it is for you in every plane of consciousness. If it is a bad dream, just take it as a mental hallucination and throw it away. If it is a good dream, remember it, but do not give undue value to the dream. That is to say, don't think of the dream all the time and forget about your reality-life, which demands your conscious and constant attention. If you can remember the dream inside your heart, it will give you joy, inspiration and aspiration so that in your reality-life you can be more devoted, spiritual, divine and perfect.

When I first go to bed, sometimes I get a strong feeling of a dream that I had the previous night. Why is this?

This means that your dream, whether it was positive or negative, was very strong. With positive dreams you go forward; with negative dreams you go backward. A positive dream is like a flower. You keep a few flowers on your shrine and they emit a fragrance. After some time, even if you take the flowers away, still the fragrance remains. You burn an incense stick for some time and you smell the incense. But when you remove the incense, the same fragrance is there. The thing goes away, but its essence remains.

A similar thing can happen with a person. If a saint stands in a certain place, then for some time after he goes away the purity, peace, joy and love that he had in him will continue to vibrate at that particular place. If a bad person full of anger and other undivine qualities stands in a certain place, then his undivine qualities also remain there and vibrate for some time after he leaves. When the person goes away, the quality that he embodies remains at the spot, and you get the effect of the consciousness that he had when he was physically present. It is the same thing with a dream that lingers after it is over. If the dream was very powerful, the essence of the dream, its main quality, remains with you.

To be in love with a sweet dream
Is the beginning
Of a blossoming, illumining
And fulfilling reality.

How can we have spiritual dreams?

If you want to have sweet dreams, inspiring dreams, then you should meditate most soulfully early in the morning—at three or four or even five o'clock. If you normally get up at five o'clock, then get up at four o'clock. Take a proper shower and then meditate for half an hour at least. Then after meditation, sit down or lie down and concentrate on your navel. Do not think of dreams at that time. Try to feel that your navel chakra is opening. Try to imagine that a wheel is there rotating very fast. Because you have meditated for half an hour, you do not have to worry if you enter into that chakra, even though it is the vital chakra. Then go to sleep for about half an hour or forty minutes. If your meditation is sound and genuine, if it comes from the very depth of your heart, any dreams you have afterwards will be divine, dynamic, beautiful, soulful, colourful dreams. They will be about angels and gods, or about your spiritual life; or you will see some encouraging, inspiring things.

If you want to have good dreams before three o'clock, please try to meditate on your navel for about ten minutes at night before you go to bed.

The navel is where emotion starts. Emotion itself is not bad; it is a question of how we use it. When we have human emotion, we only bind ourselves and others. But when we have divine emotion, we expand our consciousness. If you concentrate on your navel centre for ten minutes, you can bring the human emotion under control and allow the divine emotion to go up from the heart, upward to the highest.

So if you want to have dreams from the higher worlds and not from the lower worlds, then before you go to sleep meditate for at least five minutes on your navel centre and the centres below the navel. This you will do in order to lock the doors to these centres. Then meditate for another five minutes on your heart centre and on the centres above the heart. This you will do in order to unlock the doors to these centres. While locking the navel centre and the lower centres, try to feel the dynamic and volcanic energy of the hero-warrior. While unlocking the heart centre and the higher centres, try to feel the cheerfulness and delight of a child. If you can do this, without fail you are bound to have dreams from the higher worlds.

Can you explain more about how we should concentrate on the navel chakra?

From the navel chakra the life-energy can take two courses. If it flows downward, it enters into the lower vital. If it flows upward, it enters into the cosmic energy. All the chakras are in back of the spine, in the subtle body, but it is easier to concentrate on the front side of the body. It is easier to concentrate on the navel than on the corresponding place in the spine. While concentrating, repeat "Supreme" as fast as possible. For purity, the most immediate and effective result comes when you chant out loud so that the outer ear can hear. But this result is temporary. If you want to have abiding purity, then you have to chant in silence. If you do it out loud, each time you say "Supreme," try to imagine one hundred "Supremes" inside it, so that your mind feels that you have repeated it hundreds of times. Imagination is a world of reality. Make up your mind that you have done it and then you will be successful.

The naval chakra works very fast when it is invoked. If this chakra and the ones below the navel open too soon, then it is a real curse. But if they are opened at the proper time, then there is no difficulty. If you concentrate on other centres, you will also get dreams, but you have to be careful not to get carried away by your dreams.

Should I pray not to have bad dreams or just let dreams come that come?

First meditate on the heart and feel the real presence of light. Then take this light and throw it into the dark abyss of the navel for purification. Then you cannot have any bad dreams because your vital will be purified.

When we go to sleep, should we try to dream divine dreams or should we just sleep naturally?

If we feel that some divine dreams will inspire us because for the past few days or weeks or months we have not been able to meditate well, then it is advisable to try to have divine dreams when we go to sleep. In this case, they will be an inspiration to help us meditate as well as we once used to. But if we are only charmed by the word "dream" and want to have a dream for the sake of the pleasant feeling or pleasure it gives, then it does not help our spiritual life in any way.

Is it bad to pray for spiritual dreams?

It is not bad for an ordinary seeker to pray to God for spiritual dreams. Dreams can be inspiring, just as experiences can be inspiring. But if you do not have dreams, if you do not have experiences, that does not mean that you are not fit for the spiritual life or that you are not fit for God-realisation. There are people who think that God is displeased with them because they do not have any experiences. Far from it! God may be most pleased with them.

Suppose I want to reach a door. There are two ways of going. One way is to go there consciously. My calculating mind may say that I have to take four or five steps to get there. Each step is an experience for me. If my physical mind wants to be convinced at every moment while I am walking toward my goal, then I can say that step one is an experience, step two is an experience, and so on. But again, if I know that my destination is awaiting me, it may not be necessary for me to count each step or to have constant experiences each step of the way. What is necessary, in my case, is only my destination. I just go there and God is ready for me.

If you want to have dreams or experiences, they can serve as preparatory steps, but they are not necessary at all. The human mind always wants to be convinced and wants to get joy at every step when it does something. But if we live in the heart or in the soul, then we need not give that kind of importance to experiences and dreams.

God is preparing each of us in different ways. If He does not want to give us convincing experiences, no harm. But if we pray to God for convincing experiences or sweet dreams, there is no harm in our prayer. Eventually a day will come when we shall offer God the highest prayer: "O God, if You want to, please give me dreams. If You want to, please give me experiences. If You don't want to give me dreams or experiences, that is fine with me. Only make me worthy of Your Compassion. And if You don't want to make me worthy of Your Compassion, that is also up to You. Only do with me as You will. Let Thy Will be done in and through me. I care for nothing except for Your own fulfilment in and through me." When we have that kind of prayer within us, then God comes to us and says, "Do not be a beggar. Do not cry for dreams; do not cry for experiences. Take Me, the Reality itself."

If our consciousness is low during our dreams, is it harmful spiritually?

If our consciousness is low and unaspiring at any time, it affects the seeker in us. The kind of dreams we have when we are in a low consciousness are detrimental to our inner life. If we have dreams from a low plane of consciousness, the best thing is to meditate more sincerely, more devotedly, more soulfully on the following day. In this way we can prevent these undivine dreams from entering into us again. Unaspiring dreams cloud our mental sky, damage our aspiring and dynamic vital and even try to destroy our physical health.

When we have bad dreams, does it mean that wrong forces have entered into us?

Sometimes before we go to sleep we eat food that is not good for us. Then it is not because of wrong forces that we have bad dreams, but just because of the food which has entered into our system. Also, if we have wrong thoughts while eating, we may think that it is all over; but it is not. At night those wrong thoughts may create bad dreams. So bad dreams are sometimes caused by food and sometimes they are caused by what we think while we are eating.

If you sleep with your hands joined together on your chest, over your heart, you will sometimes get nightmares. It is best to sleep either on your side or on your back and not to have any pressure on your chest while you are sleeping. Sleeping with your hands on your chest is not at all good. You may sleep for many hours, but you won't sleep well. Also, it is not good to cover your face with the blankets or sheets.

What should we do if we have a frightening dream?

When you have a frightening dream, please do not give it undue importance. You may dream that something bad is going to happen in your life. But if you are disturbed or frightened by the dream, then that in itself is already something bad. Suppose you have a dream that a friend or relative of yours will pass away. Your dream may be absolutely correct; tomorrow he will surely die. But if you are frightened now, then today he is already dead for you. If you surrender to the dream, you will suffer unnecessarily before the actual hour. Also, your fear will immediately enter into the future victim and create an additional burden for him.

On the other hand, if you are not frightened, then during the time that lies between your dream and the possibility of its occurrence, you can fight against it through prayer and meditation. Instead of being frightened, try to offer your prayers to God. Perhaps you think that prayer is something feminine or delicate. No! Your prayer is your greatest strength. God's strength is His Compassion and man's strength is his prayer. If you can meditate, that will be an even mightier strength. If you pray and meditate sincerely and God's Grace descends, I assure you that you can delay the actuality of any prophetic dream. Many times it has happened that spiritual seekers have dreamed that their relatives were going to die, and immediately they started meditating and praying to God. Then, God's Grace descended. God does not always nullify the possibility, but He may delay the actual event.

Why does God help the aspirant in cases like this? God helps because God is not bound by cosmic law. Since cosmic law is created by God, at any time He can break His own law. If He cannot break His own law, then He is not omnipotent. And you can make God break His law through your soulful prayer. God says, "This is to be done." He has recorded it. But when human prayer enters into His Heart, He may cancel His own decree.

Is it possible to transform a bad dream into a good dream?

While you are having a bad dream, if you really want to transform your bad dream into a good dream, then you must immediately try to wake up. Stand up and stretch your limbs; then sit down and meditate. If you dive deep within, then the strength of your inner meditation and light is bound to transform your bad dreams into good, illumining and fulfilling dreams. This is what you have to do if you want to transform them. But if you want to get rid of the bad dreams, then get up immediately right after you have had the dream and say, "Ah, I am now relieved from the evil attack." Before you go back to sleep, smile and laugh and dance because the attack is over.

If you often have bad dreams, you have to be more careful, more conscious, more devoted to your spiritual life, especially during the time of meditation. Each time you meditate, you should feel that the results of the meditation are like a river flowing toward the sea, its destined goal. When you have a bad dream, feel that the dream is not the goal. It is only part of a journey. During the journey you may encounter foul weather and obstructions on the way, but if you are brave, you will inevitably reach your destination.

So be brave during your dreams and feel that the dream is not the end. If you have an unhappy dream, feel that it is a necessary step that will strengthen you in your spiritual life. Needless to say, Reality itself is crying for your arrival at its door. It desperately needs you, your heart's cry and your life's conscious and constant oneness, so that it can manifest in and through you for life-perfection and love-manifestation on earth.

Why is it that I may have a wonderful meditation, and then that night I have impure vital dreams?

When you have vital dreams, it means that your vital has to be purified. If you leave your room messy, you cannot expect to enter into the room and find that all of a sudden it has spontaneously become clean. You have to enter into the room and try to clean up the mess by putting away some things and throwing away other things.

During your meditation you are receiving light. When this light enters into your being, it may show you that your vital needs purification. If you enter into a dark room without a light, you won't see anything, and you may think that everything is all right. But once you turn on the light, you will see that nothing is all right, that there are all kinds of destructive forces in the room. This is good, because then you will be in a position to transform these forces. When you get peace, light and bliss from your meditation, you have the possibility of entering into your vital and purifying it. So when you have a powerful meditation, try to bring the light from your meditation into your vital. Then your dreams will be purified by the power of your meditation.

How can we gain more control over purity in the dream state?

In the waking state you have some control over purity, whereas when you are sleeping, you have practically no control. But this is a matter of practice. If you want to become a good musician, you have to practise, practise, practise. Then you can play all the tunes perfectly, right from the beginning to the end. But if you don't practise, you are bound to make mistakes. If you want to become a good dancer, you have to practise the steps day in and day out; otherwise, you will never be perfect.

In this case also, if you can meditate on purity most soulfully and if you can be perfect in your inner life during the day, then I assure you that you will also be perfect even while you are fast asleep. Once you have purity in your dreams, you will be most satisfied, because dream represents reality and reality represents dream. What you dream is a reality in some other world, a higher world or a lower world. If you can have some mastery over impurity in the physical world, then I assure you that in the dream world also you will have mastery over your impurity.

Does the soul gain any experiences to help its evolution from negative dreams, as it does from real experiences in life?

"Negative dream" is a very complicated expression. A positive dream we know is something that is inspiring, something that is aspiring in and through us. But negative dreams can be of various types. If, because of a lack of aspiration, somebody dreams about the lower vital life, sexual life, these dreams do not help the soul at all. But if one dreams that he is trying to do something, such as study, but he is failing in his examinations, or he wants to run towards the light but he is not able to move his feet, these kinds of negative dreams can be beneficial. These negative experiences, these temporary pangs, will not stand in one's way as they might if they were experiences in the outer life. One suffers for five minutes, but when he wakes he is determined to do the thing and to be successful. New determination and new aspiration enter into him and he becomes stronger and more powerful.

We have to take these kinds of dreams as experiences which are helpful at times to make us strong. The son of a boxer is fighting with his father. The father is teaching him how to box, and all the time, the father is striking him and knocking him down. Or a wrestler is teaching his son how to wrestle and the son is being pushed and shoved. These experiences of the buffets of life do help the soul, because they make everything that composes one's existence—the physical, vital, mental and psychic—strong in the battlefield of life. These experiences can help the soul by strengthening other parts of the being. The stronger we are in our integral existence, the more opportunity our soul gets to work through us for the manifestation of its own light.

Negative dreams of this kind can definitely help the soul, just as dreams of progress and success can help the soul. If the dream is just about success in the vital world, the soul does not gain anything. But if success is achieved by virtue of one's divine qualities, one's sincerity and devotion, then the soul gains. And if the dream is of progress in the spiritual life, that dream can definitely offer substantial help to the soul if we give it proper importance.

If you have a good dream about someone, should you tell the person?

When you have hopeful dreams, illumining dreams, encouraging dreams, when you see that something significant is going to take place in a friend's life, you should consciously try to identify your soul with his soul. How will you do this? Through your meditation. He will eventually get joy from the event because it belongs to him. But this joy, by God's Grace, you have received before he has. If you are wise, you will go deep within and assimilate the joy that you have received and then try to offer it to him inwardly before he gets it directly from God. Otherwise, if you tell him, "I had a wonderful dream about you," he will be happy for a second, and then he will doubt you. He will say it is all your mental hallucination. Despite your best intention, his doubtful mind will throw cold water on your encouraging message. So instead of telling the person verbally, try consciously to offer him the joy of the dream through your meditation. At that time, he will get additional strength. Before he gets the experience of your dream, which may or may not come to him in the form of reality, he will start getting inner peace and inner joy which he will not be able to account for, because you have started injecting him, preparing him to receive something very high, very meaningful and fulfilling. Similarly, when you have good dreams about yourself, go deep within and prepare yourself to be ready, to be a fit instrument to receive the reality as it should be received.

If in a dream we feel deep love for someone, how can we best carry detached love into our outer relationship?

If we feel deep love for someone in a dream, first we have to know whether or not this love is emotional love. If it is emotional vital love, then immediately we have to offer both our love and the object of our love to the Supreme in us.

This kind of dream is like eating cake. First we try not to eat the cake at all, because of the weight problem it will create for us. But if we find that we have to eat the cake, then we do so secretly. We are afraid to eat the cake in public, for fear that the world will see us and laugh at our greed, so we do it secretly. But the best thing is not to eat the cake at all, not even in secret.

If inwardly we consciously do something wrong, then it is very difficult, almost impossible, to detach ourselves from it. Therefore, we should always try to be fully alert so that in our dreams we do not do the things which we should not and would not do in our waking hours. We can be fully aware in our dreams by developing more conscious will power in our waking hours.

Can we derive any benefit from writing down our dreams each morning?

You can derive much benefit from writing down your dreams in the morning provided that they are good dreams, illumining dreams, encouraging dreams, fulfilling dreams. Each dream is like a flower on a tree. Each flower adds to the beauty of the tree. When you have a good dream, feel that your life-tree has borne a flower, a flower of joy, a flower of gratitude, a flower of beauty or a flower of peace, which can be placed at the Feet of the Supreme. If you have inspiring dreams, you can write them down either on a piece of paper or on the tablet of your heart. Then when you are sad, depressed or disappointed, if you read your inspiring dreams, they will immediately elevate your consciousness to the highest height.

It helps to write down your dreams, but you should not analyse them with your mind. If you use your mind, all the subtle essence of the dream will vanish immediately. All its importance, meaning, glory and capacity—everything that is divine and essential in the dream—will be taken away. So do not use the mind. Do not analyse and scrutinise; only keep the dream inside your heart. Cherish it and treasure it. Then if you become a victim to negative forces, think of your good dream. At that time if you look in the mirror, you will see how divine you have become.

The power of a dream
Can make a man
Unquestionably happy.
But the power of a reality
Can alone make a man
Unreservedly perfect.

What is the best way to learn the meaning of our dreams?

It is very difficult to give the proper significance of dreams. As there are seven higher worlds and seven lower worlds, there are also many dream worlds. If someone sees a dream in a particular world, then its significance there will be one thing, and if he sees it in a higher dream world, that will be a totally different matter. Each plane has to be known and understood properly. Each plane offers truth in a particular way.

Many books have been written about dreams. Each one has its own way of explaining dreams. If you read books for the interpretation of dreams, each book will give a different meaning for a similar event. There cannot be any standard explanation of dreams because you have to know from which plane the dream is coming.

If you don't have a spiritual teacher, you have to dive deep within in order to know the real significance of the dream. Try to feel your own existence inside the dream; try to feel that you are inside the dream itself. Those who meditate daily will not find it difficult to do this, because when we meditate regularly, we widen our consciousness. If the significance doesn't come to you either from within or from a spiritual teacher, the best thing is to continue to aspire. The time will come when either you will find a teacher who can help you, or your inner being will teach you the significance of your dreams.

If you know the real significance of a dream, then naturally you will get the inspiration to go forward in your spiritual journey. If you have a wonderful dream and if someone properly explains it to you, then you will get more inspiration to go deep within. Sometimes you may have a frightening experience in your dreams and you think this signifies that something bad is going to happen to you. That may not be true. Perhaps the dream indicates the death of your vital life or emotional life. That is why it is good to have a spiritual Master who can guide you in this respect. Then you will know the true significance of your dreams. If you have good dreams, inspiring dreams, you will get the strength of an elephant to go forward, because you will feel that your progress has been inwardly ordained. You can get real benefit only from the proper explanation of your dreams.

When a baby smiles or cries while it is sleeping, is it because it is dreaming?

When babies smile while sleeping, it is the soul expressing its joy in a visible way in the face. The soul feels joy that once again it has the opportunity to fulfil its promise to the Supreme. Then the psychic delight immediately expresses itself on the child's face.

There are various reasons why a baby may cry while sleeping. At a particular hour he may be hungry or thirsty. Another reason is that the child may be having a dream. A child between the ages of four and seven will have dreams almost every night. When we have dreams that are destructive, frightening or tormenting, we do not usually cry aloud. We know that we will be alarmed only for a few minutes or seconds. But in the child's case, the child feels that he has been attacked, and he does not know what the attack is or when it will be over. He feels that if he cries aloud somebody will come and save him.

Can dreams at such an early age be reminiscences of previous lives?

Sometimes they are reminiscences of previous lives. Also, if other members of the family are fighting, or if people in the neighbourhood are fighting, the vibrations remain in the atmosphere. Then the child may suffer because he is the weakest in the family. Consciously he may not even know of these fights, but if his parents are fighting or if his brothers and sisters are fighting, these wrong vibrations may enter into the child's consciousness, and the child may suffer.

What is the spiritual difference between dreaming in colour and dreaming in black and white?

Dreaming in colour signifies different phases in one's life, different types of consciousness in one's life, either progressive or destructive. Dreaming in black and white signifies the union of darkness and light, of night and day, of negative, destructive forces and positive, constructive forces.

What does it mean when you see colours in a dream?

Each colour has a spiritual significance. In a dream you may not see any person or hear any words; you may just see flashes of light. When you see light in your dreams, you have to know that this light is going to enter into you and manifest in you and through you. When you know the meaning of this light, immediately you will be able to interpret these dreams.

When you see a pure white colour in your dream, immediately you should know that divine purity and the divine consciousness of the Mother is entering into you. The Universal Mother has all colours, but pure white light happens to be Her dearest colour and it is through this colour that She manifests Herself. So Her consciousness will come as pure white light.

Similarly, if you see a pale blue colour, you have to know that it indicates Infinity, spirituality and great power. Green indicates new life, vitality and dynamism. If you see green light, it means that new life has dawned. When you see the colour red, you will know that divine power is entering into you.

What is the significance of flying in a dream?

Sometimes you will dream that you are flying like a bird or an airplane at your sweet will. You are soaring from rooftops, touching the earth and then rising up again. You may think that these dreams are coming from the higher worlds, for if you are able to fly, this must mean that you are on a very high level. But, in fact, dreams about flying take place only in the higher vital world. We do not fly on the mental plane or any other plane, but only on the higher vital plane. If you have dreams of peace and light, if your whole consciousness is inundated with peace, light or beauty, this kind of dream is taking place inside the soul's region and not the vital.

What is the significance of falling in a dream?

A dream of falling has three possible meanings. When you fall, if you are frightened to death, it means that your consciousness has become totally one with your vital being. This kind of dream takes place on the vital plane. If you are falling and enjoying the fall, like a child playing on a trampoline, it means you are becoming one with the aspiring reality that is below you and around you. This kind of dream takes place on the psychic plane. If you see, while falling, that many human beings are looking at you from below with an eager hunger, that means you are bringing down light from above to feed aspiring humanity. This kind of dream is unusual and, at the same time, most significant. It takes place only on the soul's plane.

Often I dream that I am falling off a cliff, and that immediately wakes me up. What does this mean?

This kind of dream can be interpreted in two ways. Either you are being energised by a divine force to dive deep into your being to illumine your body-consciousness and to fulfil God in all parts of your being, or an undivine force is compelling you to fall down from the height you have attained because it does not want you to enjoy the bliss of spiritual height. When you fall, if you are not frightened to death, if on the contrary you feel tremendous energy to do something for the Supreme on the plane where you have landed, that means a divine force is operating in and through you. If you are frightened, however, that means you have been assailed by a wrong force. So I advise you always to pray and meditate in order to be inspired and guided by the divine forces for the total illumination and perfection of your life.

What is the significance of oceans, rivers and other bodies of water in dreams?

Water signifies consciousness. When we dream of water in the ocean, it means consciousness in its immensity, in its vastness. In a river, consciousness is dynamic. A river is movement, movement toward the destination. When we dream of a river, we have to feel that consciousness is flowing toward its destination, which is the vast ocean.

What does it mean when you see animals in a dream?

Animal dreams generally take place in the vital world, but no matter which plane of consciousness your dream comes from, if you see a deer and the deer is running, this indicates that you are running very fast in your spiritual life. If you see an elephant in a dream, no matter on which plane the dream takes place, you have to feel you are being energised with enormous strength in your spiritual life. If you see a dog biting you, this means that you have lost faith in your spiritual life, in your Master and in yourself. But if the dog is following you, this indicates that you have absolute faith in your Master and that you are your Master's obedient disciple.

What about fish?

The occult significance of fish is meanness. But again, fish can encourage people to swim in the sea of knowledge and wisdom. If you see a beautiful fish swimming, you are seeing the water-consciousness, and that may mean that the fish is inspiring you to swim in the sea of knowledge-light.

What does it mean when you dream that you are injured or in a battle?

When you dream that you are injured or in a battle, it means that you are being attacked by some undivine forces. These forces may attack you on the physical plane, the vital plane, the mental plane or even the psychic plane. The attack and the injury may take place on any plane. But when you see it, it is your mind that sees it, and it is the mind that convinces you that you are injured. When you have a dream that you are in a battle, if it is on a higher plane, that means you are fighting against ignorance. If it is on a lower plane, it only means that your own undivine life is fighting against somebody else's undivine life. If you are a spiritual seeker, if you dream of a battle, that usually means that you are fighting against ignorance. You have already taken the side of God, truth and light, so you are fighting against the forces that are standing against you, against your highest realisation of light and truth, against your revelation and manifestation of the divinity within you.

If one has a dream about one's spiritual Master, is it reliable?

Unfortunately, it is possible for wrong forces to take the form of a great spiritual figure or a spiritual Master and appear in a dream. At times they are successful and they do many bad things. How can you distinguish the real Master from the hostile forces? When a wrong force appears in a dream in the form of a spiritual Master or a great saint, the first thing you will notice is its impurity. If you see there is no purity, then immediately you will know that it is not the Master, but a wrong force in the form of the Master. Many times it has happened that negative forces have taken a divine form and appeared before a seeker, and the seeker bowed down to these wrong forces. You must never, never bow down in a dream unless and until you are sure that that particular person is really your Master or Krishna, Christ, the Buddha or some other great spiritual Master. Otherwise, the moment you bow down and touch the person's feet, occultly that wrong force will take away some of your divine qualities.

When you see a Master in a dream, first see if he brings with him a flood of purity and the fragrance of a flower or the radiance of light. This purity can never be brought by the wrong forces. The moment you feel absolute purity and the fragrance of flowers, you can rest assured that it is a divine person who has come. But if you feel impurity or if you are alarmed or frightened, then you can be sure that it is an impersonation by a wrong force.

If I dream that you tell me something, how can I know if it is true?

If I tell you something in a dream, first of all you have to know whether it is actually I who have said it. Sometimes it happens that mentally you create a figure of me. No hostile force can take my form, but imagination can be very strong. You may create from your own wishful thinking a being with my face, my body. Like a painter, you may create me and make yourself feel that it is I who have said certain things. If you create that kind of Guru with your wishful thinking, it is not really I who am giving you instruction. But if you have meditated and prayed during the day, and at night I just appear to you unexpectedly and give you a message, and if your heart is thrilled, then you will know that it is I. If you are ready to jump out of bed with the capacity and inspiration of a lion, or even if I scold you in the dream, you are thrilled, then you will know that I have given the message to you. But the thrill has to be in the heart, not in the mind or the vital. If you see me in a beautiful or luminous form, it is genuine.

If you mentally create me, at that time you may doubt the experience. Your own soul will enter into the false dream and warn you. But when you have a pure dream of the highest order, you will not have the capacity to doubt it.

If you see me vividly and if it is something very solid and distinct, then if I give you some message, it is as good as my giving you the message on the physical plane. But if it is a serious matter, it is better for you to clarify it with me. Otherwise, it may create real problems. It may be wishful thinking. If your dream is genuine, I will immediately say so.

When a spiritual Master finds it difficult to offer a message to a disciple on the physical plane, it may happen that it is easier for him to offer the message on the inner plane in a dream. When the disciple comes to the Master on the physical plane, the disciple immediately sees the physical in the Master. At that time, he may not think of the Master as the Highest for him. But on the inner plane, where there is no mental barrier, the disciple may see the real height of the Master, or at least he may see more of his height than he can see on the physical plane. At that time the disciple may have more faith in the Master's words.

I often dream of you. Sometimes I feel that it is really you, but sometimes when I get near, I don't feel your vibration.

My vibration is very complicated. I don't have the same vibration all the time. Sometimes it is a compassionate vibration and sometimes it is a dynamic vibration. Sometimes it has dynamic power to such an extent that it may seem that I have become ferocious enough to destroy you. But that power is not aimed at you. On the contrary, it enters into you to challenge and destroy the wrong forces that have attacked you. Last year you had to have an operation. If the doctor had only caressed your hand, would you have been cured? Similarly, when you see me in a powerful consciousness, feel that it is necessary. Sometimes I come with love, compassion, concern; but I also have other vibrations.

No hostile force can take my form. Hostile forces have taken the forms of many spiritual Masters and have deceived their closest and dearest disciples. When I appear in a dream, it is one of my divine forms. The form I take depends on your inner needs.

What happens when we dream about you?

When you dream of me, all your beings are fed with joy, even though the outer being may not get the result for a day or two. But if you don't have any dreams about me, that doesn't mean that you have made no progress. If you meditate well, you will get the same result. But if you see me in a dream, it is a good sign. It is not that I shall only praise you. Sometimes I may scold you. As I scold outwardly, I can also scold inwardly. In that case, you should feel that it is for your good that I am doing it. When you dream of me, it is another opportunity for you. Those who live near me see me so many times in the physical world. But the dream world is also a world where people can approach me. If you see me in a dream, it often means that your heart or soul has made a special effort to commune with me. Or it may happen that you have not made any effort, but I have come to you because I feel that your heart needs some special attention.

If you dream of me, that means you are actually receiving one part of my being. When you see me in a dream, part of your physical being, part of your vital being or part of your mental being is receiving me. Or it can be the whole physical being, vital being or mental being that is receiving me. But if your physical being still has impurity in it, it may be frightened to receive and welcome me. The vital being may be frightened because of its aggressive and stubborn qualities. The mental being may be frightened because of its obscurity and lack of wideness. But once you have made considerable progress in the spiritual life, the moment you receive me with your physical being, you will feel a sense of tremendous joy—the joy that awakens you and makes you aware of the world within and the world without. If the vital being receives me, you will feel that you are marching and running toward your destined Goal. And if the mental being receives me, then you will feel that you are flying in the sky of Infinity and Eternity.

When we have a dream about you, are you aware of it?

When you dream of me, it means that a part of my being or an emanation of mine is in touch with you. My physical mind may not know and need not know what is happening, but an inner existence of mine is definitely aware of it. If something very important, serious, significant, dangerous, alarming or illumining has happened or is about to happen in your life, then the emanation or inner being of mine is bound to bring the message into my physical mind either that morning or during the day. But if it is only the kind of divine nourishment that you usually get, then the being need not or will not bring it to my attention. When you dream of me, it is either because I want you to have the dream so that you will receive something special, or it is because of my soul's love for you.

When you come into the dream of someone who is not yet your disciple, what does it mean?

If a spiritual Master comes to someone in a dream, it means that the soul of that particular person has already recognised the Master. Like a magnet, the soul is pulling the Master's love, concern, blessings and affection. The soul is pulling the presence of that Master. Perhaps a few days or a few months later, the physical eyes will be able to see the Master. The soul has recognised the Master on the inner plane, and it has transmitted this truth, this reality, to the dream consciousness. From the dream consciousness, in the course of time, the reality will come to the physical plane. It is a very good indication that sooner or later the person will be able to meet his Master.

Who can dream?
Who is dreaming?
Who will always dream?
Only the God-lover
In the seeker's aspiration-heart.

I had a dream that my mother was going to die. I knew it, so I prayed and prayed. Then she did die.

Your dream was preparing you. If you hadn't known, your shock and your sorrow would have been more severe. When your mother's death took place, on the one hand you were very sad, but on the other hand your dream had already helped you to become stronger.

I had a dream about my older sister. She was wearing a green sari and she was standing on a path at twilight.

Green means new life. If your sister was wearing a green sari, it means that new life, new hope has entered into her.

Now, there are two types of twilight. One is early morning twilight and one is evening twilight. Which one was in your dream?

It was the evening twilight.

The green sari means inspiration, dynamic energy, new hope, new identity, new life, and twilight means half light and half darkness. Although your sister has hope and inspiration and cries for new life, she is not fully ready to accept the spiritual path. She is ready to have fifty percent darkness and fifty percent light. If she were really aspiring, she would want to have one hundred percent light. She has or had the opportunity to be dynamic, to be very fresh and full of enthusiasm, and to enter into the sea of light, but she did not care for the opportunity. She did not avail herself of it. She wants to enjoy both the outer world of darkness and the inner world of illumination at the same time, which is impossible. She wants half light and half darkness in her life, a mixture of both. But a mixture of both cannot fulfil her.

Once in a dream I saw a very ancient temple where lots of people were worshipping statues. I recognised all the faces I saw. What is the significance of this?

These were the people whom you knew in your previous incarnations. This kind of dream makes you feel that this is not your first or your last incarnation. You were something and you knew some people before. If they were not good people, then you will know better people in this incarnation. It encourages you in this way. If you have not done something in the past, you can do it now, and if you don't do it now, you can do it tomorrow. This is the purpose of reincarnation—so that if you have not done something, you will be given the opportunity to do it in another life.

If you saw an uninspiring person in the street yesterday, and today in your dream you see that person again, what benefit do you get? When you saw him yesterday, you didn't get anything. By having a dream of that person, you still don't get anything. But if that particular person was very spiritual, sincere and aspiring, then you got inspiration from him when you saw him. And at night, if you see the same person in a dream, then you get additional inspiration. If you see aspiring people, it is a blessing. But if you see unaspiring people during the day, it is a waste of time, and if you see those people at night, it is also a waste of time.

I had a dream that you told me to make a blue ball for you.

Blue signifies something very vast, something infinite, and a ball means the world or the Universal Consciousness. The blue ball here represents the eternal instrument. I was telling you that the Supreme is making you a dependable instrument of His.

I dreamed that I was talking to someone and we were looking over a vast, fertile land. I saw a sky which was like a golden dawn, with the sun rising over the land and casting a gold light.

The sky signifies vastness. And the vast land that you saw also represents vastness. When the vastness above and the vastness around you meet together, only then will fulfilment come. The higher vastness means Heaven, and the other vastness is earth, where you are living. When our earth-consciousness is widened, immediately the Heaven-consciousness, which is infinitely wider than the earth-consciousness, meets with the earth-consciousness. When they meet together, you see a gold colour. This is the colour of divine manifestation. When earth is receptive, when earth's heart is wide, then the light of Heaven can enter into it. At that time, Heaven's illumining consciousness and earth's aspiring consciousness become one. And when they become one, it is a manifestation of the divine Reality.

I dreamed of a very lustrous, bright orange serpent. What does this mean?

This dream of yours was very significant, but the colour that you saw was not orange; it was gold. The colour gold signifies divine manifestation. A snake means energy. You will see snakes around Lord Shiva's neck, symbolising the energy that is around him. Each snake has a meaning of its own. If they are not black, then they are all good. If you see a black snake, you have to know that it is an undivine force. But if you see a snake with a golden colour or a red colour, the gold signifies divine manifestation and the red signifies power. A gold snake means the manifestation of divine energy. Divine energy entered into you, into your spiritual life, and it wanted to flow through you in the form of manifestation.

I dreamed that I was outside my parent's house and I saw an old friend of mine whom I had known before I became your disciple. He brought back a sort of bad state in me, but I was playing with him. All of a sudden a large, powerful purple eagle came down from the sky and attacked me. I killed it, and I felt the most powerful force that I have ever felt in myself.

An eagle flies high, but its consciousness is very low. It is like a seeker who pretends to be in a high state of meditation, when actually his consciousness is in the lower vital or in the gossip world.

When you saw your old friend, who was still in the consciousness that you had before you entered into the spiritual life, your old undivine life suddenly came forward and attacked your spiritual life. The undivine life has a kind of arrogance and a feeling of superiority. It is not only the divine life that feels it is superior. The life of aspiration feels that it is the real life, but the undivine desire-life also feels that it is the real life. Your previous life was the life of desire; there was no aspiration in it. Although you used to lead a very unaspiring life, inside you there was a feeling of superiority.

You felt superior to people who were not doing as you were doing. You felt that either they were all fools who were not experiencing anything in their lives or they were cowards who were not brave enough to enter into the adventure of life. That kind of pride you had. Just as the eagle flies high but has a very low consciousness, so also you were proud, haughty and arrogant, although your consciousness was on a very low plane.

Then all of a sudden, because you accepted the spiritual life, your soul came to the fore. Since you accepted the spiritual life soulfully and consciously, your soul used its power and destroyed the eagle. The eagle represented the false way of climbing. The soul wants you to climb up and soar above, but in a true way, with aspiration, and not with desire, arrogance and a negative, destructive feeling of superiority. It was your soul's light that destroyed your undivine qualities in this dream.

I felt that I was climbing a very steep hill on luscious, green grass. It was becoming very steep, and I was afraid, but I kept going up with the assistance of an unidentified person. Just as I was about to reach the top, I was distracted by some nuns offering flowers.

I wish to say that the spiritual path is most arduous, and it is very steep. When you have to go up, it is most difficult. The beings you saw were not actually nuns; they were angels. But in your dream you felt they were nuns because your physical mind was operating. Your physical mind did not want you to see angels, because it did not want you to get the greatest joy. The mind is like that. It destroys everything. With your heart you went up very high, but your mind wanted to diminish your joy. So the mind made you see them as nuns. If the mind had not interfered, then you would have been so happy to see angels with flowers.

I had a dream in which all I saw was your face. It was very powerful and dynamic, and it came right in front of me and seemed to be pulling me.

This dream means that it is necessary for you to accept life powerfully and courageously. You have entered into a new life, and there is a subtle fear in you. I was pouring tremendous energy into you in this dream. This energy was entering into you and, at the same time, like a magnet it was pulling you. Through my concentration I made a conscious entrance into your soul so that you will not have fear. It is necessary for you to be powerful and dynamic so that you can receive an abundance of truth, light and bliss in your new life.

I dreamed I was sinking down into something, and when I came out it was like coming out of meditation. I almost wanted to stay there.

It was not actually sinking. You went very deep within. You entered into the region of your soul for real rest and fulfilment.

I had a dream in which I heard distant music, and when I woke up I thought I was either dead or in Heaven.

This was a most powerful experience that you received from the depth of your soul. The music that you heard was from the soul. This music cannot be appreciated by the outer ear; it has to be appreciated through our inner organ.

In the ordinary life, when the lower vital or emotional vital does not appreciate or identify with something, immediately we feel that we are dead. When the body and vital do not appreciate the soul's music, they are dead to that kind of music which inspires and elevates our consciousness. So when the physical is separated from the soul—the soul's music, the soul's light—the physical is spiritually dead. It is not that you are dead, but when the unaspiring body does not accept the soul as its source, then we feel that it is like a dead soldier, just as we say that whoever does not practise spirituality at all in his life is a dead soul.

I had a dream in which I entered a room. I saw that you and all your disciples had wings.

Wings mean that the disciples have soaring aspiration. They are not the wings of an angel or the wings of a bird, but soaring aspiration that flies very, very high, infinitely higher than a bird. It is absolutely true that my disciples are most sincerely trying to develop and increase their power of aspiration. Disciples who aspire definitely have these inner wings, which are called aspiration.

I dreamed that I fell down through the earth and become a prisoner somewhere. Then a group of us, myself and other prisoners, had to try to work together to get out of the prison.

That prison is the prison of inconscience, where there is no light, no hope, absolutely nothing positive. The prison of inconscience is the land of destruction. You have come out of it just because inside you there is something very sincere, very soulful, very devoted. So the unconditional Blessings of the Supreme have entered into that inconscience and brought you back. You have come out of it because the divine Grace, the unconditional Grace of the Supreme, has saved you.

I had a dream about Krishna and Arjuna. In the dream felt that I was Arjuna. The word "Arjuna" came out of my stomach.

Krishna and Arjuna have the very closest connection with each other. They are spiritual brothers. Arjuna signifies the inner instrument, and Krishna represents the Highest. So Krishna wants you to be a real divine, detached and surrendered instrument of the Supreme. To be Arjuna means to be the dearest, most effective, most faithful and devoted, chosen instrument of God. The voice that came from within means you identified yourself with Arjuna's consciousness. That is to say, you wanted to be as powerful, as devoted, as surrendered to your own Master as Arjuna was to Krishna.

I dreamed that I was carrying a large box along with someone else, and I was taking it to you. Then you came and said that I was not doing the right thing.

You were unconsciously taking the responsibility of someone else and bringing it to me, and I was telling you that it is the wrong thing to do, because that person does not want to give you or me his responsibility. You feel that it is your bounden duty to bring me the load, which here means some person who is involved in your life. You wanted to bring that person to me, and I was saying that the hour has not come for that person to follow our path. For him it is only a bother and nothing else, for he is not ready for the spiritual life, especially for our path. If you go deep within, you will know who the person is.

For several mornings I have heard a bird singing beautiful music, like a flute, during my sleep. But when I wake up I cannot remember the music.

This bird is your soul, and the music is coming from your soul. When you are asleep your consciousness has a free access to your soul. But when you wake up you come back to your ordinary life and cannot retain this free access because your physical consciousness is not in touch with your soul. If you have a very powerful meditation before you go to bed, then you will be able to retain the soul's consciousness the following morning. During your meditation try to feel that you are not the body but the soul and, at the same time, that you exist for the soul. Then you will easily be able to remember the music of your soul-bird.

Once during a dream I felt that Socrates and Ben Franklin were two incarnations of one soul. Can you trust a dream that seems so clear?

It depends on your development. Today you are thinking that Socrates was Benjamin Franklin; tomorrow you may think that he was Aristotle, and many other names may go through your mind. If it is simply an ordinary dream or a kind of a mental flash, then please don't give any importance to it. But if it dawns like a vision, then you can say that it is something true, and you will derive benefit from it.

Why can dreams sometimes be more inspiring than reality?

Every human being is of the opinion that a dream is infinitely more inspiring than reality. The immediate effect of a dream on our mind is to create inspiration. This is because when we are in the dream world all our soul's capacities are at our disposal. We can do many things and see many things which we cannot do or see during our waking hours. We can freely enter into many realms which we cannot enter at other times. When we develop the inner capacity to enter into all these realms at will, then we will see that dream and reality have become one. At that time reality and dream will be equally inspiring.

Is it possible for a spiritual dream to be as beneficial as meditation?

There is a kind of dream which amounts to vision. If you have a dream that indicates an imminent new dawn, a new birth, this kind of dream is nothing short of a vision, and it is as good as a high meditation. This kind of vision or reality is an indication of great progress in our life's journey toward the ever-transcending Beyond and in our life's mastery over the ignorance-sea. If you have that kind of vision, if the Supreme wants to, He can give you partial realisation. Such a dream is not only as good as meditation, but far surpasses meditation.

We are nothing short of
God's own Dream
That is being unfolded
For the transformation of earth's
Ignorance-life
Into Heaven's perfection-light

What is the difference between human dreams and God's Dream?

There is a great difference between human dreams and God's divine Dream. Human dreams are only mental fantasies. Most of the time they are just pensive thoughts, ideas or fabrications. Sometimes we become victims of hostile forces which make us dream all kinds of horrible things. Again, sometimes we create our own fantasies which come in the form of dreams during the night.

God's Dream is the divine Dream which is the precursor of Reality. God's Dream embodies Reality itself. It is like a cover or lid on a jewel box. You just lift the lid, and there inside is the wealth: gold and diamonds. With His Dream God is entering into the world of His fulfilment, which is the constant manifestation of Reality. The highest Reality is the transformation of human nature, which is right now half animal and half divine. The highest Reality will be manifested here on earth, but it will take quite a few centuries. That doesn't mean we can remain silent and inactive—far from it! If every day we consciously sail in God's Dream-Boat, then slowly, steadily and unerringly this Dream-Boat will take us to God's Reality-Shore. This Reality-Shore is not somewhere in Heaven; it is here in our day-to-day life, in our thoughts, in our actions, in our very existence on earth.

About The Author

Sri Chinmoy is a fully realised spiritual Master dedicated to inspiring and serving those seeking a deeper meaning in life. Through teaching of meditation, his music, art and writings, his athletics and his own life of dedicated service to humanity, he tries to show others how to find inner peace and fulfilment.

Born in Bengal in 1931, Sri Chinmoy entered an ashram (spiritual community) at the age of 12. His life of intense spiritual practice included meditating for up to 14 hours a day, together with writing poetry, essays and devotional songs, doing selfless service and practising athletics. While still in his early teens, he had many profound inner experiences and attained spiritual realisation. He remained in the ashram for 20 years, deepening and expanding his realisation, and in 1964 came to New York City to share his inner wealth with sincere seekers.

Today, Sri Chinmoy serves as a spiritual guide to disciples in some 100 centres around the world. He advocates the "Path of the Heart," as the simplest way to make rapid spiritual progress. By meditating on the spiritual heart, he teaches, the seeker can discover his own inner treasures of peace, joy, light and love. The role of a spiritual Master, according to Sri Chinmoy, is to help the seeker live so that these inner riches can illumine his life. He instructs his disciples in the inner life and elevates their consciousness not only beyond their expectation, but even beyond their imagination. In return he asks his students to meditate regularly and to try to nurture the inner qualities he brings to the fore in them.

Sri Chinmoy teaches that love is the most direct way for a seeker to approach the Supreme. When a child feels love for his father, it does not matter how great the father is in the world's eye; through his love the child feels only his oneness with his father and his father's possessions. This same approach, applied to the Supreme, permits the seeker to feel that the Supreme and His own Eternity, Infinity and Immortality are the seeker's own. This philosophy of love, Sri Chinmoy feels, expresses the deepest bond between man and God, who are aspects of the same unified consciousness. In the life-game, man fulfils himself in the Supreme by realising that God is man's own highest self. The Supreme reveals Himself through man, who serves as His instrument for world transformation and perfection.

In the traditional Indian fashion, Sri Chinmoy does not charge a fee for his spiritual guidance, nor does he charge for his frequent concerts or public meditations. His only fee, he says, is the seeker's sincere inner cry. He takes a personal interest in each of his students, and when he accepts a disciple, he takes full responsibility for that seeker's inner progress. In New York, Sri Chinmoy meditates in person with his disciples several times a week and offers a regular Wednesday evening meditation session for the general public. Students living outside New York see Sri Chinmoy during worldwide gatherings that take place three times a year, during visits to New York, or during the Master's frequent trips to their cities. They find that the inner bond between Master and disciple transcends physical separation.

Sri Chinmoy accepts students at all levels of development, from beginners to advanced seekers, and lovingly guides them inwardly and outwardly according to their individual needs.

Sri Chinmoy personally leads an active life, demonstrating most vividly that spirituality is not an escape from the world, but a means of transforming it. He has written more than 700 books, which include plays, poems, stories, essays, commentaries and answers to questions on spirituality. He has painted thousands of widely exhibited mystical paintings and composed more than 6,000 devotional songs. Performing his own compositions on a wide variety of instruments, he has offered a series of several hundred Peace Concerts in cities around the world.

A naturally gifted athlete and a firm believer in the spiritual benefits of physical fitness, Sri Chinmoy encourages his disciples to participate in sports. Under his inspirational guidance, the international Sri Chinmoy Marathon Team organises hundreds of road races, including the longest certified race in the world (1,300) miles, and biannually stages a global relay run for peace.

Sri Chinmoy's achievements as a weight lifter have also earned him considerable renown. To demonstrate that inner peace gained through meditation can be a tangible source of outer strength, he has lifted objects weighing as much as 7,000 pounds using only one arm. In addition, he has honored more than 1,700 individuals by physically lifting them overhead on a specially constructed platform in an awards programme entitled "Lifting Up the World with a Oneness-Heart."

For further information, please write to:

AUM PUBLICATIONS
86-24 Parsons Blvd.
Jamaica, N.Y. 11432

Additional Titles by Sri Chinmoy

Meditation: Man Perfection in God-Satisfaction

Presented with the simplicity and clarity that have become the hallmark of Sri Chinmoy's writings, this book is easily one of the most comprehensive guides to meditation ever written. Some key topics: proven meditation techniques that anyone can learn, how to still the restless mind, developing the power of concentration, carrying peace with you always, awakening the heart centre to discover the power of your soul, the significance of prayer . . . plus a special section in which Sri Chinmoy answers questions on a wide range of experiences often encountered in meditation.

$9.95

Beyond Within
A Philosophy for the Inner Life

"How can I carry on the responsibilities of life and still grow inwardly to find spiritual fulfilment?"

When your simple yearning to know the purpose of your life and feel the reality of God has you swimming against the tide, then the wisdom and guidance of a spiritual Master who has swum these waters is priceless. In this book, Sri Chinmoy offers profound insight into man's relationship with God, and sound advice on how to integrate the highest spiritual aspirations into daily life.

Topics include:
• The spiritual journey • The transformation and perfection of the body • The psyche • Meditation • The relationship between the mind and physical illness • Using the soul's will to conquer life's problems • How you can throw away guilt • Overcoming fear of failure • The purpose of pain and suffering • Becoming conscious of your

own divine nature • The occult • and much more
$10.95

Death and Reincarnation

Now in its 9th printing, this deeply moving book has brought consolation and understanding to countless people faced with the loss of a loved one or fear of their own mortality. Sri Chinmoy explains the secrets of death, the afterlife and reincarnation.

Topics include:
• *Overcoming your fear of death* • *Is death painful*
• *Postponing the hour of death* • *The truth about reincarnation* • *How to help those who are dying*
• *The soul's journey after death* • *The meaning of Heaven and hell*
$5.95

Kundalini: The Mother-Power

En route to his own spiritual realisation, Sri Chinmoy attained mastery over the kundalini and occult powers. In this book he explains techniques for awakening the kundalini and the chakras. He warns of the dangers and pitfalls to be avoided, and discusses some of the occult powers that come with the opening of the chakras.

Topics include:
• *Developing occult power* • *The significance of the different chakras* • *Concentration and will power* • *Mantras to awaken the kundalini centers* • *Opening the heart centre* • *Sexuality and occult power*
$5.95

My Daily Heart-Blossoms

Spiritual Meditations for Every Day of the Year

In this series of 365 spiritual illuminations—one for each day of the year—Sri Chinmoy leads the reader to the inner wellspring of light from which all truth comes.

These aphorisms, poems and reflections have a familiar ring that resonates in the mind and heart long after they have been read and absorbed. They are at once simple and supremely profound . . . wisdom spilling over into poetry . . . and poetry that will carry you to new heights of realisation.
$9.95

Inner and Outer Peace

"A powerful yet simple approach for establishing peace in your own life . . . and the world."

In this book Sri Chinmoy speaks of the higher truths that energise the quest for world peace, giving contemporary expression to the relationship between our personal search for inner peace and the world's search for outer peace. He reveals truths which lift the peace of the world above purely political and historical considerations, contributing his spiritual understanding and inspiration to the cause of world peace.
$7.95

Eastern Light for the Western Mind

Sri Chinmoy's University Talks

In the summer of 1970, in the midst of the social and political upheavals that were sweeping college campuses, Sri Chinmoy embarked on a university lecture tour offering the message of peace and hope embodied in Eastern philosophy. Speaking in a state of deep meditation, he filled the audience with a peace and serenity many had never before experienced. They found his words, as a faculty member later put it, "to be living seeds of spirituality." These moments are faithfully captured in this beautiful volume of 42 talks.

Topics include:
• *The inner voice* • *The quintessence of mysticism* • *The secret of inner peace* • *Attachment and detachment* • *Self-knowledge and self-control* • *The ego* • *How to please God* • *Fear of the inner life* • *God and myself* • *Individuality and personality* • *The body's reality and the soul's reality* • *Intuition* • *Perfection* • *Consciousness* • *Inner poverty*
$6.95

A Child's Heart and a Child's Dreams —
Growing Up with Spiritual Wisdom
A Guide for Parents and Children

Sri Chinmoy offers practical advice on a subject that is not only an idealist's dream but every concerned parent's lifeline: fostering your child's spiritual life, watching him or her grow up with a love of God and a heart of self-giving.

• *Ensuring your child's spiritual growth* • *Education and spirituality—their meeting ground* • *Answers to children's questions about God* • *A simple guide to meditation and a special section of children's stories guaranteed to delight and inspire*
$5.95

The Master and the Disciple

What is a Guru? There are running gurus, diet gurus and even stock market gurus. But to those in search of spiritual enlightenment, the Guru is not merely an 'expert'; he is the way to their self-realisation. Sri Chinmoy says in this definitive book on the Guru-disciple relationship: *"The most important thing a Guru does for his spiritual children is to make them aware of something vast and infinite within themselves, which is nothing other than God Himself."*

Topics include:
• *How to find a Guru* • *Telling a real spiritual Master from a false one* • *How to recognise your own Guru* • *Making the most spiritual progress while under the guidance of a spiritual Master* • *What it means when a Guru takes on your karma* • *Plus a*

special section of stories and plays illustrating the more subtle aspects of the subject
$5.95

God's Hour

Daily Meditations for Spiritual Living

Each of the 365 aphorisms in this book may be read as meditations: tools for quieting the mind and fortifying the heart which will inspire you in your personal journey toward self-perfection. Read the aphorisms meditatively and you'll find that they create a healing inner image. They will show you that your potential is far greater than you may ordinarily choose to believe. Each aphorism becomes a guide for the day, a source of inspiration and a signpost toward truth.
$6.95

The Summits of God-Life
Samadhi and Siddhi

"Essential reading for all seekers longing to fulfil their own spiritual potential."
This is Sri Chinmoy's firsthand account of states of consciousness that only a handful of Masters have ever experienced. Not a theoretical or philosophical book, but a vivid and detailed description of the farthest possibilities of human consciousness.

Topics include:
• *What is Nirvana* • *How to accelerate your God-realisation* • *The highest consciousness known to man* • *The Sat-Chit-Ananda consciousness*
$5.95

Astrology, the Supernatural and the Beyond

Sri Chinmoy describes the unseen forces that operate in and around you. You'll learn to welcome the positive forces while protecting yourself from the negative ones.

Topics include:
• *Prophecy* • *Occult power* • *Black magic* • *Psychic power* • *The spirit world* • *Mediums* • *Spiritual healing* • *Life on other planets* • *Flying saucers* • *Hostile forces*
$5.95

Mother India's Lighthouse
India's Spiritual Leaders

Thirty essays on India's greatest souls. A beautiful introduction to the philosophy of the East as manifested through India's greatest poets, philosophers, scientists, politicians and saints.

Topics include:
• *Gandhi* • *Sri Aurobindo* • *Rabindranath Tagore* • *Sri Ramakrishna* • *Swami Vivekananda* • *Nehru and more*
$1.95

Yoga and the Spiritual Life

Specifically tailored for Western readers, this book offers rare insight into the philosophy of Yoga and Eastern Mysticism. It offers novices as well as advanced seekers a deep understanding of the spiritual side of life. Of particular interest is the section on the soul and the inner life.

Topics include:
• *The meaning of Yoga* • *Understanding the law of karma* • *Self-knowledge and universal knowledge* • *Reincarnation and spiritual evolution* • *The ego* • *Using mantra and japa to develop purity* • *The synthesis of East and West* • *Discovering your soul's special mission* • *and more*
$5.95

My Flute

This collection of Sri Chinmoy's poetry conveys the whole spectrum of spiritual emotions ranging from the doubts and fears of the wavering pilgrim to the ecstatic realisations of the illumined Master. Sri Chinmoy, in his role of seer-poet, writes with a power, lyricism and authenticity seldom encountered in this genre. $3.00

The Music of Sri Chinmoy

Flute Music for Meditation

While in a state of deep meditation Sri Chinmoy plays his haunting melodies on the electric echo-flute. Its rich and soothing tones will transport you to the highest realms of inner peace and harmony. An excellent aid to meditation and relaxation.

(Cassette) $9.95

Inner and Outer Peace

A tapestry of music, poetry and aphorisms on inner and outer peace. Sri Chinmoy's profoundly inspiring messages are woven into a calm and uplifting musical composition with the Master chanting and playing the flute, harmonium, esraj, cello, harpsichord and synthesizer.

(Cassette) $9.95

Ecstasy's Trance
Esraj Music for Meditation

The esraj, often described as a soothing combination of sitar and violin, is Sri Chinmoy's favourite instrument. With haunting intensity, he seems to draw the music from another dimension. The source of these compositions is the silent realm of the deepest and most sublime meditation. Listen to the music and enter this realm, a threshold rarely crossed in the course of one's lifetime.
(Cassette) $9.95

Silence Speaks

Sri Chinmoy plays the cello and flute. He also sings while accompanying himself on the cello and harmonium. This recording captures the intensity of Sri Chinmoy's unique style of devotional music.
(Cassette) $9.95

The Dance of Light

Sri Chinmoy Plays the Flute

Forty-seven soft and gentle flute melodies that will carry you directly to the source of joy and beauty: your own aspiring heart. Be prepared to float deep, deep within on waves of music that "come from Heaven itself." Comes with a free booklet on music-meditation. (Cassette) $9.95

■   ■   ■

To order books or tapes, request a catalogue, or find out more about Sri Chinmoy or the Sri Chinmoy Centres worldwide, please write to:

Aum Publications
86-10 Parsons Blvd.
Jamaica, NY 11432

When ordering a book or cassette, send check or money order made out to **Aum Publications.** Please add $1.50 postage for the first item and 50¢ for each additional item.